I0518023

Advance Praise for
Fire Season

You want a poetry book with poems that sling you from where you sit or stand to the stars, to the blood and yelps of midnight coyotes on mesas, to the bear's claws raging over the carcass of a mountain lion, to a mother's tears and a father's sorrow as mean and incendiary as it gets and can get to the growling human heart that is capable of sustaining grief but barely, barely this, barely these poems, then read this book and find yourself among the pages of a real poet with words that really count and words that are made of skin and spirit and tears and silence...the stuff of journeys....

—Jimmy Santiago Baca

People wonder who "the numbers are" in prison. As Jeff Knorr tenderly, angrily, hopelessly, hopefully reminds us: it is sons and daughters, parents and children. *Fire Season*, a metaphor for both the crisis of his son's incarceration, and his son's firefighting, offers a glimpse of what the absence of the prison system creates in those left behind: longing, guilt, regrets, and ultimately, surrender. In tender, beautifully wrought poems, Jeff brings us close to the fire, and to the love, showing us the boy inside a troubled man, the man inside a troubled system, all while addressing historical violence against Black and Brown bodies, and grappling with his own whiteness in relationship to his son and the new foreign land he's entered. In sensitive, but bold and inventive poems that map the correctional landscape from multiple angles and views, we see cages, yards, the empty home. We see, in every corner, the search for the "small gods" that might take mercy for each of our mistakes. These poems teach from the heart, about the system, about relationships, about forgiveness.

—**Caits Meisner,** Editor of *The Sentences That Create Us: Crafting A Writer's Life in Prison* and Past Director, PEN Prison & Justice Writing

FIRE SEASON

FLOWERSONG
PRESS

poetry by

JEFF KNORR

FlowerSong Press
Copyright © 2024 by Jeff Knorr
ISBN: 978-1-963245-01-1

Published by FlowerSong Press
in the United States of America.
www.flowersongpress.com

Set in Adobe Garamond Pro

No part of this book may be reproduced without
written permission from the Publisher.

All inquiries and permission requests should
be addressed to the Publisher.

NOTICE: SCHOOLS AND BUSINESSES
FlowerSong Press offers copies of this book at quantity discount with bulk
purchase for educational, business, or sales promotional use. For information,
please email the Publisher at info@flowersongpress.com.

table of contents

Section 1

Section 2

Section 3

Section 4

for my son and all families who've endured
the violence of the justice system

No condoms for the heart

Violence, H. Rap Brown proclaimed, is American as apple pie

Over 6 trillion served; over 2 million behind bars

—C.D. Wright,
from *One Big Self*

FIRE SEASON

1

"I could wake up in the morning
without a warning
and my world could change:
blink your eyes.
All depends, all depends on the skin,
all depends on the skin you're living in."

—**Sekou Sundiata**,
from *Blink Your Eyes*

After the DA Makes an Offer, We Counter and Wait

I'm fishing today, casting into the river of my blood
  looking for a silver flash, hiding behind that boulder of my heart.

I tie on a new fly and wish for you upstream
  knee-deep in this green ribbon—loops casting, casting.

You've tied your anger, the way I have,
  like this tiny clinch knot at the end of the hook.

Only we can undo this—it will remain like that until
  we're broken off by a tremendous fish.

The sky speaks of winter, streaked with clouds, and you
  hope, the way pines wait for new snow.

And these flakes each in their own pattern; they'll never know.
  But geese rend this dark wind, as a birth an opening.

In This Country Everything Might
Swallow Us

for my son

On the north coast near the redwoods
we sit eating barbecued oysters
washed down with beer where the tide
pulls into the bay hard, swelling
like my fear as I sit across from you watching
watching flocks of brant disappear into fog.

Occasionally the sun breaks through.
On the other side of the highway
the pulp mill churns, its smokestacks stinking
the air. Log trucks hammer the afternoon
with their jake brakes slamming against
the salt and fog coming down the grade.

Could there have been another way?
After dinner at Lou's on the bay
When we walk down Main street
side by side, I bump your muscled shoulder,
your hair and jaw-line give away the young
man who is the only one that knows
how these shadowed days falling
on us will all turn out.

The tide swirls. The moon will find
the water tonight push against it,
creating chopped waves. We'll search
the dark water under the pier for answers.
What kind of promises could we make
to keep from being swept out
into all this glimmering light?

Tattoo

1. Parents

It started with *Brenda* across your smooth left pectoral muscle,
the first one, the script you said you did yourself in a mirror.

Just that empty muscled chest and her name, your birth
mother still in Guatemala, far from us now, love inked into you.

Bird songs lost into mornings; clouds dissipate into sky;
when we throw stones at the lake, after the ripples vanish

the lake is smooth again; but those stones settle on the bottom.

At the Schoolyard

The sun is on my back as it burns down in the sky.
The day is closing out like drawn curtains.
I'm wishing you were here now, with us, the dog and me
tossing the bumper into the green carpet of grass in the schoolyard field.
It's not like fields where we chase birds, flushing roosters,
but right now the dog and I want you
right here, your musky smell and smile, firm
hands that swing the bead always on target
against the rooster veering away toward the slope of the draw.
There's just too much cement and wire around you now
and not enough tall grass, sunlight, and wind.
But when you're here with us next, we'll
chase the roosters like girls, whistle to the dog
to hold and flush, and finish the day in the dusk
on the tailgate, the way we always have;
you giving me lessons on how to shoot
and me burning the sunset and your face into my eyelids
like the glowing end of your cigarette against the dark.

Ain't No Faces in Tables and Graphs

The local paper comes and on page 3 is an article and statistics about crime, the safety of our neighborhoods. Mostly it just reads like all the others, some stories and facts and then I look to the side and see the table and map, crimes committed and where, and there you are on that map, in that table. There's no lining up who you are with you being one of those statistics, but you are and there's no denying that, no denying where I have to drive to see you, no denying your X-reference number that takes the place of your name. People wonder who the numbers are. Every one of them somewhere, waiting for a letter to fall in like ducks. For the warmth of sun on the back. Waiting to feel water flow around bare ankles, stones under feet. Waiting for the visit that may or may not come. You said to me one day sitting in fire camp, pines clothing the ridge and the steel gray clouds hammering up the canyon—*everybody's here because of dope, dad.* So, we build more beds and walls way out among cactus. Among forests. Beyond pasture and wild land. So the same wind brushing past slow cattle and alder trees carries the names away. Leaves numbers where nobody knows to look

From the Official National Midterm on White Oppression and Corrections

337. They are all white, all middle-aged, and all men. A few live openly lavish lifestyles, but the majority fly under the radar. Rarely is there news about them in the mainstream media or even the trade press. They are obscure CEO's who are
    a) manufacturers of HVAC systems
    b) window companies so we can all have a better view
    c) hotel companies
    d) gun manufacturers

14. They have kept their heads down and their fingerprints off regulations designed to protect their businesses—foremost a law that shields gun companies from liability for crimes committed with their products are
    a) gun manufacturers that own the top ten largest companies
    b) selling firearms in the U.S. which profit
    c) after every mass shooting in the country
    d) because the NRA tells us guns keep us safe

77. If, at dinner, your Mexican-American mother-in-law raises, not her glass, but the question, *what does the NRA sell, anyway?* Look at her like she has brought flowers to the dinner and then rather seriously you say
    a) rose-colored glasses,
    b) membership to the largest cult in the world,
    c) and a brand of fear and hate some white folks just love to buy

133. If your son yells down the driveway, *I'll shoot you motherfucker* after you've stepped into an argument he and his girlfriend are having which has already blasted apart the quiet of your neighborhood like a semi-automatic, your own breath rising in the cold like smoke from the barrel, he
    a) is likely on meth and so out of his head
    b) he will not remember what happened,
    c) but feel contrite about it when you confront him after the meth has worn off,
    d) looking 12 again, sad and lost in those glassed eyes

Eclipse

Will the moon ever move off this spot on my heart,
       what I hope you'll never have to know?

The way the rancher feels, even old, lifting
       the razored knife against the calf he's raised.

You say you'll never come back to the house—you can't
       after your old man called the police to take you.

I saw you cry in the back of that car.
       Then sleep took you over until the cruiser rolled into booking.

The young boy in you comes, maybe running
       with our old shepherd your cape bright against the sky or swinging

the rope swing on the sycamore in front of the house or
       hiding in the corn maze while I chase you.

All things turn dark this time of day,
       the way the sun is blotted by the moon

and the air chills; a breeze blows and the birds go quiet.

Sometimes You're Still in the House

The dark watermark of your absence, a hush.
—David St. John

In the last sun of the day, I'm still holding you
like a Maidu woman who has lost a child
and collects pine needles and feathers
carrying this swaddled sack of earth
speaking to it until she knows the soul's
connection to the other world. You see,
even though I know where you are, I'm still asking
for you, speaking as if you can hear me
like the day you lay in the soft, wet dirt of our duck blind
sleeping at my feet while I whispered to you
and the passing birds. On some distant slope
your heavy boot prints in the scorched earth
from last fire season bloom with lupine.
Do seasons really return a charred
landscape back to something beautiful?
Sometimes your childhood questions of the world
stay with me and I answer them again, long for another,
ask a father's questions of clouds and fire.

Horses

This September morning the grey sky
      blankets the valley and unrolls itself
           as far away as you.

If you could go outside the drops would brace
      your skin the way the rain cools me this hour
           without a shirt and out with the dogs.

I dreamt last night your face was gaunt
      your skin pocked like a chiseled sidewalk.
           You lay back on the concrete sticking

a syringe of heroin in your arm many times.
      How I cannot save you. How not hearing
           your voice in weeks makes the mind

run like horses. All of you branded with numbers,
      in those cells like stalls, the halls of ghosts,
           the silence we all fear on the outside.

Our National Treasures

"I say we had better look our nation searchingly in the face, like a physician diagnosing some deep disease."
—Walt Whitman from *Democratic Vistas*

We the People of the United States of America stand accused of the wrongful action of resisting the law when the law is wrong and being brown in the wrong place and time and *O, say can you see* that the writing is on the wall for anyone who wants to try to have a conversation when you're getting pulled over. No, instead, put your hands in the air like you just don't care, you know the routine—license and registration. N*o person shall be deprived of life, liberty, or property* except now we can Google the Innocence Project and see the names and faces and know that's not true. And, Oh, my Lord, tell me how we let sweet Emmet Till die for doing nothing but talking to a young girl who passed at him first. His mama had the courage to open that casket and people drove some darkened roads to get there and stand in line for hours to see that young man. In America *excessive bail shall not be required nor excessive fines imposed* but what does that mean to the homeless. Tell that beautiful tale to the family living in the old section of fill-in-blank city now called the hood or the barrio or the white down and outers whose kid was picked up for having meth and a pipe and maybe a gun and has a 250k bail. Let us look in that mirror at our sallow faces, our deep-set eyes, sunken in the sockets because we're sick and sick and tired of losing ourselves to the disease. Turn the lights on. Let's call the good doctor. Let's get our mind right. Diagnose this sickness for what it is, not what it feels like, not what we think it is because the President or Congress said so, but because it's too easy to say *that big brown man coughed on my neighborhood and made me sick.*

Longing for My Incarcerated Son
While Walking The Ranch Near
Dunnigan, California

His body rolls brown
like these dry wintered hills,
   the muscled ground

      presses against the skin of earth.
I could walk the acres
      of his body like this ranch

      we've hunted, searching
all these empty rivulets
      and graveled ditches

      each saddle running toward a draw
where pheasant tuck in and
      hide the way he does

      behind the tall grasses of fear.
It is all I can hold to wonder
      what has been disked beneath

      the surface, to wonder what
will grow back on that long
      expanse scorched by fire.

Disappearing Them

"We enhance public safety through safe and secure incarceration of
offenders, effective parole supervision, and rehabilitative strategies
to successfully reintegrate offenders into our communities."
—Mission Statement, CDCR

Sixty-six thousand employees watching over the fences.

We never get sent to good places, and even if
  it's good outside, ain't nothing good about prison.

Ironwood, Blythe California; Corcoran SP, Corcoran, California.
  California Medical Facility, Vacaville, CA; Avenal State Prison;

California Substance Abuse Center, Norco, California.
  There's really a town called Norco? With a substance abuse center?

California Correctional Center, Oh Little Suzy,
  and High Desert State Prison, Susanville, California,
    Oh, Susanville, Restore The Night Sky

remember the call for the jobs and now Walmart has shut down
  your small stores and Burger King and Taco Bell came
    even before the prisons were finished.

What is taken away is immeasurable and only shows in the eyes
     empty as the Blythe desert around Ironwood.

183, 928 inmates today and every facility but one
     over one hundred percent capacity.

Have you ever had a dog?
     I did. His name was Dutch and he used to hunt
          with me and my pop 'til my pop left and took the dog too.
          Guess he liked that dog more than me.

North Kern State Prison, Delano, California.
     Total Population: 4,105. Design Capacity: 2,694. Staffed Capacity: 3,911
How much gasoline until a match catches?

Wasco State Prison. Mule Creek SP, Ione, California.
San Quentin, oldest prison in California, built by the
     inmates themselves, skilled labor.
          Million Dollar Marin County View at the Q.

Pleasant Valley State Prison, Coalinga, California.
     Is there anything pleasant in that valley?
          Lord I walk through the valley of death…

I had a sister once. Still do I guess, but she
     quit coming to see me five years ago.

DVI, Tracy, California whose walls have seen
     the reception of the hundreds of thousands.

Old Folsom, long remember Johnny Cash.
    Singing in the chow hall, OG's still talk about that.

That boy ain't been right since he got here.
    Probably never will be again.

Twelve billion dollar budget.
    Sixty-six thousand employees.
        The California Department of Corrections operates
            thirty-five adult prison facilities and forty-three camps.

Sadness has been riveted to him like an airplane wing.
    Do you know how many rivets are in a cell door?
        You would if you were in a cell.

California Department of Corrections and Rehabilitation: Dial 1 to be Connected to Visiting

I would just like to hold you, the way
I might hold a horse in the pasture.

Please listen carefully: for instructions in English Press one
para Español oprima dos

I listen for your voice in hushes deep as lakes.

Please listen carefully or visit our website
as rules and regulations have changed
for visitation and acceptable clothing

I will wear or not wear whatever they tell me
and your grandmother has gone down the road
to Walmart for a new bra without an underwire.

If you would like to speak to a representative
stay on the line or visit the VPASS portal
on the CDCR website to make a visiting appointment

Ok, Saturdays at 10:30, it's scheduled,
we'll count each visit like marbles that roll away.

Father Fire Blackbirds Wind Son

If I could clean your heart, release you
like a wing-shot pheasant catches wind.

Catching the roar of fire and wind,
I closed my eyes, looked toward the sun.

Looking toward the sun the confused father
is trapped in the heat you know as your own fire.

Trapped in the heat and confused as water,
There were thousands and thousands of blackbirds.

There were thousands of blackbirds tossed like dice
and the house was quiet, your room empty.

The house was quiet, your arms were prison strong.
Outside, I saw my own blood, police lights.

Police lights, your eyes locking with darkened truth.
Kneeling, if I could clean your heart, release you.

2

"We were all running down demons with our
Chests out, fists squeezed to hammers and I was
Like them, unwilling to admit one thing:
On some days I just needed my father."

—Reginald Dwayne Betts,
from *Bastards of the Reagan Era*

Green Dot

We spit these digits over the phone
     Like we're throwing around birthdays
or phone numbers and apparently

nobody's listening because the CO's
     never crash your bunk to see what's there.
You ask for $50 but I always slip one more

green card off the rack because I can't cook you
     French toast for breakfast, a grilled
cheese in duck fat, drink a beer with you

after walking deep hills. It gets us by—
     brings the edge off the wait,
cools you from the inside, a radiator of smoke

where the heart idles smooth.

Cell Block

You always tell me you prefer cell living to dorms. There's more privacy, less people fucking with your shit. You use your *car* to shoot lighters, cigarettes, a bag of pruno. And somehow I can imagine how it feels better to be there. When does the sun come through your small framed rectangle of window? When does the son come through my framed rectangular door? When? Door? Come? So(u)n? Window? Our lives stretched so far apart. | | | | | | Bars. These are bars. [ ] Cell. this is a cell. I want to hold you again like you were two. Two in my arms. Can we sit by the pool outside? Let me cook you an omelet, your favorite. Your dog will sit alongside you remembering your smell. He sleeps on your bed at night. I know he hates the bars too. Even

```
though he doesn't know      l  l  l  l  l  l      what a cell block is: is
a cell block what any of u   o  o  o  o  o  o      s know, but you—all of
you who have had to li       c  c  c  c  c  c      ve in an  8   x   10
rectangle, rectangle 8 x 1   k  k  k  k  k  k      0—Eighty square feet
of space, space of lonline   e  e  e  e  e  e      ss space, your space,
space—it's hard to call th   d  d  d  d  d  d      at space when most
of it's taken up by sink, toile b b b b  b  b      t, bunk, locker, unlock
all the doors. Where's th    e  e  e  e  e  e      e master button to
buzz all the American cell   h  h  h  h  h  h      block doors open. De
carcerate the State of the   i  i  i  i  i  i      Union is not good—
we are locking up childre    n  n  n  n  n  n      n--pulling families a
part like piecing out a cow  d  d  d  d  d  d      until the cow no
longer resembles a cow b     b  b  b  b  b  b      ut something we can
bare because we're buyin     a  a  a  a  a  a      g the lie that this is
working. This is not worki   r  r  r  r  r  r      ng. You are not a
number. You are a name.      s  s  s  s  s  s      You are my son. All
```

you are sons of other sons and daughters. Oh America, Oh America it hurts me to see you this way. Your ribs show. Your glassed eyes and dark circles as though you've been at the pipe too long. Once you held us, maybe in the oh purple plains and dark hearted majesty of the 13th Amendment rebuilding The South on the backs of black men, any one who broke The Law and it was your way to enslave. And now you can't take it anymore and nor can we, you see, O say can you fucking see? Where are we going? We know where we've been. Do not shackle my son anymore, drag him to the cell, lock him up like he's a danger—he's smiling in his 3rd grade photo.

Tattoo

2. Place of Birth

GUATEMALAN PRIDE arcs across
your chest from side to side that
green-black, homemade ink in ornate
letters arches the way the country
bends from west coast to east coast,
the highlands rising toward your throat
in the middle, *lago Atitlan* somewhere near
your sternum. Your birthplace, the hardened
land, the fog, the jaguar you feel running
inside, this land you've never been back to
that colors your eyes, your hair,
that runs in your blood like *los rios*,
the Mayan face of *Kichigonai*, sun god
you wear on left and right clavicle as your
muscled, brown neck reaches toward clouds.

Cut It Down: Limb It, Buck It, Burn It

Some nights here in the valley
I imagine as the honkers pass that you can
hear the snow geese moving south to Honey Lake.

Maybe in the moonlight I know you're
robbed of right now is some answer
to one of your prayers fluttering in on the scent of desert sage.

Go ahead and light these last years on fire,
let the slash pile of pain burn itself down then
scatter it, spread those embers cold, but not until
you've read the message in the ashes

Before Disappearing with Angels

In the light you never looked so sorry,
I mean, really, I've looked at you more
than I've looked at the sky and could
tell you much about who you are.

But in the trees where those blackbirds
rest is the story of angels, a story thin
as mist that only appears in morning.

You remember the horses, the way they looked
at you then lowered their heads, muzzles,
manes falling like water along their necks?

See, I know you'd question this, but I think
of you more often than a lover thinks of
the other—you might ask why, and you'll see.

∽

The blackbirds return every afternoon to the trees
        with the same permanence as the ones inked on your chest.

Then they fly toward the treetops, the sky looking
        like the birds flying toward your muscled shoulders.

I've never wanted to be a bird until now that you're gone.

We barbecued steak, I brought soda, macaroni
salad, I smuggled in even a little tobacco.
Across the table, the sun streaming off the pine
stacked ridge above struck your face.
You looked so sad, so handsome for a moment,
for a few hours you could let down
that left hand poised to block the next swing.

We ate and you said, *so I take this guy*
to see some buffleheads paddling around
and he thinks they're penguins. I'm laughing
but this is dark as hail-filled clouds, as pond water.
Then we find the horses and rub them over the wire fence—
he's never seen a horse—here's this vato scared shitless, dad—
of a horse.

On the third Thursday of March
         a letter comes from you. So I pour

a little whiskey and read it on the porch.
         Later, just a little drunk, I read

it again, then again, and cry in the dark—
         not hard, just tears running because I can

barely stand that everything now
         between us is a surprise,

as distant as Pisces in the deepening sky.

One Night

But not just any night,
on the 26th floor of the New Otani Hotel
the night of your aunt's wedding
your new uncle and I threw centerpieces,
beautiful flowers in glass volleyball-sized
vases out of the window of their hotel room
in downtown L.A. We dropped them, in
amazement, the air flattening petals of roses,
the baby's breath. They blew out
like cannon balls on the sidewalk—
flowers, soil, Styrofoam, glass. Ten times
we could have killed someone with one of those
centerpieces, our drunkenness—
it could have been over as soon as it started.
Your aunt's anger flared hot as a brand.
We could be wearing the same prison orange.
I escaped some wild death, manslaughter
by wind, by stupid luck, but you on the other hand
drive the car through our neighborhood,
stop for a cigarette with friends, have brown skin--
you ride, get pulled over, the cops
looking for you and your brothers.

Your Cartoon

You look at me through the smudged glass, say into the black plastic phone *I'll start taking your advice.* And, you know, you do for a while—I don't expect much or expect you to live like me. When you're out and running again off into those mad streets and women you say to me one night as we yell at each other over beer and the smoke of the barbecue in the backyard, *just be honest pops* and I say *throw her overboard.* But you tell me *I can't hit that and let her go*—I see where that roadrunner is taking you. Out into the desert. Into the wide open. You're following all spiral-eyed like Wile E. Coyote. Anvils dropping on you. Dynamite blasting. Falling off cliffs. Suspended in mid-air. You're burned, your eyes charred like Yellowstone in the '88 fires and we try to talk when you come down, *and the tongue is a small member, but it boasts of great things. How great a forest is set ablaze by such a small fire.* You talk and are here for a moment. Then gone again on the wild chase screaming into the night for your life, for your wild dreams that kiss you like the tongue of the moon and then you run through the painted tunnel of darkness that opens before you. In the morning I find a used sawzall and a hammer drill in the back of your truck. That sure as shit ought to get you another few pipe hits. Your mind is lit up like the Vegas Bellagio until you wake up in the late afternoon, worn out and a little hungry and ask me for an omelet. I make you breakfast in the afternoon and we sit by the pool talking, making sense for a moment before the program resumes again, the ACME truck rolling in to drop off the explosives for the night.

Monopoly

In Minnesota a man with an outstanding warrant was pulled over and offered officers a Get Out of Jail Free card.
　　　　　　　　　—*The Telegraph–July 24, 2017*

Un fucking believable flashes across his face when he reads the card—you'd think the guy told him he was Pablo Escobar. But, you see, this is a card we should all carry—hell, the cop carries one—you think that his driver's license isn't next to his badge so when one of his cop buddies pulls him over drunk on the highway—well, there it is you see. He doesn't get a K-9 released on him, the run and grab, bit hard at the shoulder, held, a gun to the back of his head—no, no, no dash cam rolling, no chest cam, no breathalyzer pulled out on that stop, *head home, head home, take it is easy, baby*—I like justice, we all do, we all want the guy doing something real wrong to get his, but come on, when it stops working that way, and we know it has, well then, we want the night to open up for everybody, we want the streetlights to shine evenly on that pavement of the American Dream—the long road home, past the trees and stars. Get us all out of jail free, change the bail system so my American brothers and sisters, sons and daughters, felons and the fabulous can go home to their families—not just the rich, not just the exalted, not just, not just…but free, make us all free, free us from all our skin our flesh and rotten meat, our bones. Free. Free.

After Three Months on Parole,
I Fear I've Lost You

after John Ashbery's "Just Walking Around"

The light rises through your
brown skin, the earth I want to hold.
Come back, return like the ducks we call
over our decoys in the dark morning.

The smudge, you bury deep, like the embers you
crush and clear with your McLeod,
the secret smudge in the back of your soul.
See what I see. I'd wear this night out on my knees
praying to gods I don't know yet.

Your easiness, the sharp-edged eye and cocked spring
An object of curiosity to some,
I already see you in your prison
orange, casual, laughing in the yard

Just walking around.

What name is there for you,
My son, who breaks the night with his meth-addled anger—
What name do I have for you?

Sagittarius, Corona Borealis—
In the sense that the stars have names,
that ride up from the inside,
terror of your own wild-eyed night

Ekphrasis of An Inmate

Prisoners wear: a) blue denim pants; b) blue chambray shirts
—CDCR Attire Restrictions

Nobody smiles in no mugshot, fool.
People look at those pictures thinking

why's that guy look so mean.
He ain't mean, that's just the worst day of his life.

This ain't like picture day in 3rd grade, but
don't forget he's got one of those too

tucked somewhere in some drawer with
his drawers, in some wrinkled envelope

and his Mami still loves that picture,
sweet like *aguas frescas* or *pan dulce.*

Let me ask you this as you look so hard:
Do you see the human or do you see the blue?

"I don't want to leave or get transferred
    to another prison because this one is too tough.
…I am looking for a path that weaves through rock
    and swims through despair with fins of wisdom.
A wisdom to see me through this nightmare,
    not by running from it; by staying to deal blow for blow."

—Jimmy Santiago Baca,
from *I Will Remain*

Your 9

I'll shoot you motherfucker
blasted down the driveway
before you slammed the metal gate.
Your XL hoop shorts sagging
with that 9 in your pocket.

And I know from watching you
cradle ducks after peppering them
with shot, smoothing their heads,
stretching wings into color,
stroking their neck hackle
that you'd never put a bullet in me.

It's why you walked off into black
night, took my car speedballing
into the streets, your fury
burning hot as a gun barrel.

The next morning, we ate omelets
by the pool and you apologized
for what you didn't even remember,
memory blazed out like oily
junipers popping in fires.

I just said *make sure the
numbers are filed off* though
I should have fought you for it.

Sometimes a father moves
in to put out the flames,
sometimes he lets them burn.

From the Official National Midterm
on White Oppression and Corrections

52. Male, 37, found dead in his cell and ruled a suicide:

    a) caused by the depression of interminable incarceration
    b) strangled by a correctional officer then hung from bed by a sheet

27. Battered woman arrested for prostitution detained by police at county jail:

    a) beaten by john who's looking to hurt women
    b) punched by officer who was pissed off at his wife

134. Which of these large corporations sows the seeds or kills the weeds:

    a) WalMart
    b) Sturm Ruger Corporation
    c) CoreCivic America

81. The young black state assembly member canvasing her district was treated by the police:

    a) like someone who was trying to break into houses
    b) like someone who was trying to break into houses

13. Stephon Clark was shot on his grandmother's back porch standing by that back door the way he had gone in for soda during afternoon barbecues:

    a) because he was black and trying to run away from police
    b) because young brown men can't trust law enforcement
    c) because even if they're walking home from school they might still be stopped
    d) because once they're an adolescent they are seen as a threat

236. Love was not the rising moon behind conjugal visits in prison

    a) they were a way to "calm" the black prisoners of the south
    b) so they brought women to have sex with the inmates who were considered violent

99. Recidivism and incarceration rates rise like July heat

    a) because the nation has impoverished large numbers of people
    b) and fails to treat them humanely

101. The largest gang in California prisons is:

    a) BGF
    b) Nuestra Familia
    c) La Eme
    d) Aryan Brotherhood
    e) Correctional Officers

Tattoo

3. Place of Residence

NOR CAL fills in the blank
of your stomach these letters outlined
and never filled in. You said when you first showed
me that you'd fill them, shade the letters
but I wonder if their emptiness about
all the space you feel between Guatemala
and this home now, the endless sky
where birds disappear, these ribbons of clouds
bending with blue dipping eventually into trees.
You'll always be this place—mallards and pintails,
the wetlands we walk, the mountains you've
packed and protected, sawed and scraped
to keep the flames from licking what you love
right off the earth like a wild tongue.

Epistle to Meth

You slipped into the house so quiet I didn't meet you the first few times. He'd bring you up the stairs. Into the room. Finally you had to come out. You weren't jittery at first, just shy and restless. Your dark hair falling around the thin face gave you away. Eyes wide and hazy as a glass pipe. You stayed and stayed. You finally broke out into crying in the night, arguing, blasting apart the quiet. You shattered the glass door. You took his calm. You eat backbones. Devour them the way dogs break the backs of small animals. You didn't care about his parole. You can creep into any house. Car. Hotel. Homeless camp by the tracks. It doesn't matter. The end is always the same. A gun to the head. Handing over possessions so there'll always be enough to wake up to cooking the ush. Load the pipe. Fire up the torch. It all goes up in flames. The house. The dreams. Ashes.

Re-Arrest

For 2 days after the cops took you,
your backpack sat outside the back door.
Finally, I dragged it upstairs like the corpse
of some dead animal.
On your bed I unzipped it, pulled out
your toothbrush, deodorant, wallet,
a jangle ring of keys to slip locks.
The gun and ammo gone, I sifted through
until I found your pair of *Tuff*
construction gloves balled one
inside the other like a fist,
the yellow and black stinging faces like bees,
keeping your knuckles clean,
so you could land a beating
like punching out bread dough.
I slipped one on, punched
the old lath and plaster wall
of your room to a slight crack.
Peeling it off, knuckles pink,
I closed my eyes, looked toward the sun
outside, saw my own blood, police lights,
the dim tunnel of bulbs in the cell block.

Ekphrasis of The Yard

Mule Creek State Prison, Ione, California

They are trapped in the sunlight
    walking side by side around
        the gray gravel track, brown

skin glistening their tattoos—
    a jaguar leaping across a chest
        an arc of Gothic letters

flashing 𝕸𝕺𝕯𝕰𝕾𝕿𝕺.
    Just outside the frame the white
        dudes gather inside the track

pitching dice in a circle
    tossing them like butterflies
        or a handful of salt into soup.

Past them a set of Mexicans is lined
    up shooting off burpees
        like a college football team.

Tucked inside the yellow line,
    two CO's in green lean into the shade
        against the wall of a building as if hiding.

At the far end of the yard
      against the fence two rabbits bound
           toward an inmate in his blues

powdery as the sky, kneeling
      offering a piece of apple from chow,
           whispering prayers flittering like leaves.

You Don't Have to Prove Anything to Me

What does it mean
to be tough
or to write a poem?
—Peter Gizzi

I know your fists have left bruises
on faces, the cheek a plum, ribs cracked
like sticks we use for tinder to set a mountain fire.

Before all this, your prison name and scars,
the tattooed stomach and shoulder,
mi vida loca, you're a man, just you
within you in the spaces of earth and wind
that move inside you like breath, that make
you wish in the morning dark of stars
staring back at you from the flooded rice
to leave all this to history.

Can the world swallow our sins?

The geese in their low honking V's,

beyond their distant song,
bring us home, bring us home.

Sonnet for the Defendant

Please rise, Courtroom sixty is in order.
Black brown black brown brown black black brown brown black
black brown black brown black brown black brown black brown
white brown black brown black brown black black brown black
black brown black brown black brown black brown black brown
black brown black brown white brown black brown black brown
black brown black brown black brown black brown brown black
brown black white black brown black brown black brown brown

black brown black brown brown black black brown black brown
black brown black brown black brown black brown black brown
white brown black brown white brown black black brown black
black brown black brown black brown black brown black brown
black brown black brown black brown black brown black brown.
Do you understand the charges? How do you plead? *No Contest.*

California Department of Corrections and Rehabilitations: Dial 2 for Inmate Information

What information could you possibly deliver—
        that he's safe, that the kite he put in
                for the GED has come through.

If you know the party's extension you wish
        to speak to, you may dial it at any time.

To dial his reference number
        and have a phone ring in his cell.

Otherwise hold for a representative—

        Information, Officer Medeiros speaking.

Yes, Officer Medeiros, can you wander
        over to dorm C, bed 211
                and check on my son for me?

Can you tell me what he's been fed the last two weeks?
        Can you check if the light flickering
                above his bed at all hours has been fixed,

replaced with a new bulb?
        Instead I ask, is he allowed to
                receive packages yet, new books?

When Medeiros says yes, I hang up
      go to Acces SecurePak, order
            soups, chips, cheese, everything

you need for a spread, throw in
      a pair of sunglasses. I go downstairs
            for a beer and cook the dog an egg.

Rehabilitation: The Step by Step Process

*Today's offender
is tomorrow's neighbor.*
—CDCR Division of Rehabilitative Programs

1. Offender's risk to recidivate and criminogenic needs assessed.
    Because we've added wood to the fire while they're inside,
        added a pile of isolation struck a match
            against those stones of pain and anger

2. Offender meets correctional counselor, placed into program based on
    rehabilitative needs.
        And the numbers run it all, *I'm sorry you're Level 3,
        you can't be in that program*

3. Offender may be placed in Academic and Career Technical Education.
    HVAC, GED, College classes, or on the yard
        talking about the next gig slinging dope or jackin' cars

4. Offender may receive Cognitive Behavioral Treatment programs.
    Because he's been treated as a number. Because all he's ever called is an Offender

5. Specialized programming for eligible offenders receiving long-term sentences.
    What is the wish in this program?

6. Offender can apply for a California Identification card.
    So, he can have a name again, can be seen in a picture smiling, so the state
        can still call him an Offender, so maybe he'll start to feel normal again, ever?

7. Offender may enroll in programs to help them reenter the community
   from prison.
   > Because it's so crazy in there, so far away, so much not like on the streets
   > > he needs to learn just how to come back out—ain't no rehab
   > > > taking place if he doesn't know how to come out and be

8. Parole Agent enrolls the parolee into a needs-based program.
   > There are always needs…more needs assessment…

9. Parolee successfully rejoins society.
   > They feel so proud to say this, and when it doesn't work
   > > and the Parolee becomes an Offender again, whose fault is that?

On a Map It Can All Look the Same

Your strength is the land, the trees—
pine, aspen, oak why they show
and disappear at elevations, the lupine

which you know only grows after
runoff, the ice bringing new color,
cover to hide the hard stone.

Rivers, which you always follow
to the flats where crossing
is easiest because the current slows,

how the surface tells the story of the bottom.
You can drop a tree with your growling saw
easy as rolling a cigarette even with

other trees exploding around you on fire.
Once you guided us over boulders
half snow-covered in the high sierra.

I let you lead us because I trust you—
You know which way to step, find your
footing in the rocks that wedge tightly.

Come home, find your way with that sharp eye
that knows what it means when
clouds move east or west.

A Right Hook Wouldn't Be Enough

OK, I should have knocked you out
taken your gun and dope—
that's what you say now, though
you were sprung, busted like a cheap
toy and no want to get fixed.
You would've just chased me down
the next day like the dog pins
pheasant to get it all back.

The head reels—your picture on
the mantle, the beach at 3 in
your plaid overalls, another on
the iCloud with the dog black
as coal in the winter sun—
three pheasant, and dark circles
of shadow around your eyes as if
the future is hard to see.

We walked the draws that day,
ditches, thigh-high thistle pushing
the dog. You, open like those broad
valley slopes, me worn into
like the deep creek, the wind urging
both of us to release our loss.

Christ, I'd spill the blood, cut
you open like an elk in the field
if I could clean your heart, release
you of all that want burning
like wild flames.

4

"While he was still a long way off his father saw him and was filled with compassion for him."

—Luke 15:20

The Day Starts Early Around That Place

Five am and the sun has yet to come;
    you are already off your rack
        steadily breathing into the day

push-ups, burpees for fighting shape
    the drop and lift to swing again, high stepping,
        off the edge of the bed frame like stairs

that could lift you right out.
    Your prison body is tight as a drum,
        but this time your mind is loose,

the heart unknotting itself from the tangle,
    the snag on the boulder in the wild river.
        Where have the birds gone to sleep tonight?

When you lie down, how those birds rest
    peacefully on your skin.
        Take your peace the new way you have

found, flying like a wing-shot pheasant
    catches wind for a long glide down the slope
        into cover. The only window you have to the outside glints—

breakfast comes and so does the sun,
    that slice of orange burns into your cell, your skin,
        your eyes, everything around you burning.

When the New Fields Sprout, You Walk Them to Clear the Mind

You turned your back on those bitter fields,
      walked away looking over your shoulder wondering

how many homies might be following to stick
      you more times than anyone could count.

Now the fields of alfalfa and wheat grow sweet and
      even if you can't see them, the air sings a song

to them with your name, without apology.
      What waits for you? Everything that you will love.

The old memories, leave them behind like a crippled
      duck in the reeds; let those tortured eyes dive

beneath the dark surface and drown themselves.
      Beyond the cells of cement and iron, of your body,

beyond the walls and towers are miles and miles
      of road and river, of pasture and mountain passes,

            each one of them leading you home.

Tattoo

4. Tombstones

You're asleep in the back of the police car
handcuffed and passed out after sobbing.
The cops have your shirt pulled up and
are trying to read your life off the page

of your flesh. The tombstones catch them
and they pause, sure that this must be a tag
for two murders—your mother over you, over them
and *no,* she says, *those are for dead years, for
'15 and '16 he was inside,* she tells them.

Their faces go confused as swirling water, the
white father who has called them on his brown
son in an upper-middle-class Sacramento neighbor
hood—*but he had a gun* they say. *I know that*
I say these tombstones are for dead years,

and all I see are more ahead—those stainless steel
cuffs, you asleep, as calm as when I watched
you sleep in your bed. The engine idles. They
pull down your shirt and straighten it out—

you asleep in that cruiser's back seat
wrapped up in all this summer's June heat.

Failing the Defendant

This language of numbers—it's all numbers—
    to replace a name, to replace time.
        The clock and calendar become god.

Figure it out. How do I figure it out?
    Figure it out. And the variables always seem to change.
Who owns the numbers—someone owns the numbers.

Why does the law get to own the numbers?
    Because that's how The Constitution was written.
                Rights—you got rights.

But you got no rights to the math in court.
    So why'd you teach me to show my work when
ain't nobody showin' me their work?

Measure. Measure. Measure twice, cut once.
        How many times has the judge measured?
           Is he done measuring?

And the body falls away,
    drifts in the water like a shadow.
    And then he's gone,

slipped out of the courtroom cage.
        A quick glance over the shoulder and
           the family is left in solitary darkness.

Because math has never mattered.
        In school, math is wasting time.
                        Now math is time, math is my life (time).

Where in the depth of swimming words is the meaning?
        These numbers move like dark fish that dart across the mind.
                This darkness is in us.

The head hums. The body tightens like a rope.
        There is no floating when the muscles become stone.
                Fall. He is falling. We are falling and sinking,

together, sinking, falling, failing.
                            The air has gone out of the body.
        There is no air as he falls down

the chute of the elevator from the cage to the pit.
            To the pit, the darkness of daily sentencing—
        the room after the equal sign.

Where is our work? Why are we not showing our work?

Show the god damned work.

Sunday, Non-Contact Visit, Administrative Segregation, Susanville, California

When you were young we played with those shiny
aluminum cuffs and key, you'd capture me
in your cape and take me by the nape of my neck
to the prison of your fort in the backyard.

Now when we visit in Ad Seg you come
shackled with sparking steel at ankles and wrists,
both of us without the key as you're locked in
the room slipping hands through door released to visit.

We talk for hours on the black phones smiling
to each other these teeth white as bone, before
the guards come back to drag you across the yard
under open blue sky when it all goes haywire.

In a heap you lie under them shackled in the dirt,
far away from the knife coming for you tonight.

Ekphrasis of Post Visit Strip Search

Why do we make a man
        bend over to spread his ass
                cheeks wide open as a price
                        for visiting his family?

The heart has been flayed open
        like field dressing a mule deer,
                the wound a gut shot that unzipped
                        the stomach for the regret to ooze out.

After hugging goodbye, watching the red
        sweater of his girl and the curls
                of his small boy pass through doors
                        slamming shut, the radiant tube lights of visiting,

sizzling the ceiling, he still needs
        to bend over in front of other men,
                balls hanging like fruit
                        to be picked or pressed.

The only thing left for the day—watching
        the reflection of those two beautiful faces
                who left in the dark ink-green pond of despair
                        to fall into and for a while drown.

Seeing You Even When You're Gone

Time will bring relief, you all have lied
       —Edna St. Vincent Millay

On the freeway, a cop cruiser pulls beside me in the hiss
of water—In the backseat a young man; the slouch of head,
shoulders the slump of heart on that long ride makes this
dark afternoon sadder than I can nearly bear.

And the Bible verses come as I knew they would,
closing the distance between the uncountable stars
and the bare walls of your cell—you tell me to read
Job, The Psalms. *And why does god not free the imprisoned?*

Where is the passage of the father who called the Romans
to take his son? Where is the absolution for that act?
Where is the guard who has decided to release this son
to the world? Tonight, there is no calm to close the gap

between the constellations of my guilt and the open fields
the dog and I walk, under the steel sky that has beat us all day.

66

Chukar

The embers of the fire blaze and I wonder
       how badly it would hurt to pick one up

and hold it in my bare palm. The pain I carry
       is stacks of old wood and the ember might burn

them away, leave nothing but the faint scent of smoke
       and a mound of black ash the size of our bodies.

Today I dropped the envelope into the blue mouth
       of the mailbox behind the Post Office

stuffed with a letter about forgiveness
       and cars and duck hunting which you tell me you love.

Those cupped wings in the photos,
       those flocks of teal racing against a blue

sky, freedom of air lifting wings.
       The pigeons on the yard you say, *fly*

like chukar, dad, so I follow them
       with my arm, lead them to keep my shot.

Your dog and I wait by the pool,
	blue in the night's throat

for the phone to ring, for your eyes,
	your muscled brown arms to be around either of us.

Fire Season

for my son, CDCR Inmate Firefighter,
Soberanes Fire, July 2016

The fires burn all around us.
Tonight the moon rose like an orange
over our valley. I imagine you in those flames
the whine of your chainsaw screams against

the roar of the fire and wind, a freight train of air.
This burning and the scent of smoke will stay with you,
the memories wax and wane like that orange moon,
maybe taking the place of the guy whose head

was smashed into the stainless-steel cafeteria table
or those big eyes getting bigger on the face
when the shank gets driven in. Your heart
flows like water even in the middle of flames;

you tell me you found a lizard in the forest on the line,
set him along your broad shoulders, let him recover
and crawl in the heat you know as your own fire,
your hair scented with ash now for months.

California Department of Corrections and Rehabilitation: Dial 3 To Be Connected to A Representative

You have taken my son from me in a system
      of lies and promises frail as dried twigs.
Don't tell me about what he needs as you stamp
      a number to him dividing our family, the system's formula.

I am a father who sends prayers into the night like birds.
      Who wonders if his son feels something inside the way a drum
is beat because somewhere in this valley his father is
      thinking of him from any one of ten thousand memories.

Don't tell me you're in the process of rehabilitation
      when after his return to us I'm simply glad he's still alive.
The dulled photos lay bare how his eyes have changed
      the oblivion of blown fires, of the sky at the horizon

I am a father lying awake at night while the stars and wind
      do their work—the night sky turning me toward morning,
         toward all that is stripped and curves away.

From the Official National Midterm on White Oppression and Corrections

Word Problems

492. The wavering heat off the August Roseland streets made the kids wish for gushing hydrants or the local pool, catching frogs in the last of the water in the drainage canal. If *a* is older Black Disciples member giving Yummy Sandifer a gun, and *b* is Shavon Dean jumping rope on the street, and *c* is the velocity of the 9mm bullet, and *n* is gang members having young members carry out hits because Illinois law will not try anyone under 11 for murder, solve for x:

$$a(b + c)n = x$$

501. In the absence of sentencing guidelines made public we wonder how the math will take shape. This is higher algebra. $4(x + y) - Bn = 12$ years. Solve for x, y, and if you think you can, or it matters B. Do not worry about *n* that's a variable that only the DA knows and you'll never figure out. If you like, you may take on the persona of any white historical figure who has crafted sentencing guidelines or handed out sentences and assume that 4 is the number you will multiply the sentence by because the defendant is brown. If you would like further assistance, refer to "Public Math" in the introduction to the Midterm.

I Had a Dream About You

There were birds, thousands and thousands
        of blackbirds, so many it turned the sky black
and then the sky twisted because all of the birds followed each other

    and then you stood in front of me
        in the sun, the birds flying on your
copper skin out of your chest tattoo, the ones you inked

        flying right out of the words *Guatemalan Pride*.
You took me by the hand and we walked
    into the woods where you were a child

        again and you opened your hand and showed me
an owl pellet that looked like a mouse, so we pulled
    back the fur and looked at all the tiny bones so frail it was hard

to imagine they were the skeleton of any animal.
    There were more birds and a truck. We drove and you slept.
    I could hear your breath. I heard your heart beat

        as if I was holding you when you were small.
When you woke you said, *I shot someone, I had to* you said, they had guns
    I had a gun. You can't tell anyone, you said.

Then a deer lay on the narrow shoulder of the road so we stopped
    and when I turned it over, wet because it was raining,
    it was a man in jeans and a hoodie and you said *that's him*

so I unzipped his sweatshirt and it unzipped his body
and your gun and a copper bullet were inside his belly.
I said, *it's ok. I don't think you did this.*

You held me in the moonlight after the rain stopped and
said *it will be ok, I am ok, dad.* Your eyes
were dark and your arms were prison strong, the birds flew

toward your shoulders again and blackbirds watched from the trees.
You told me not to worry about them. In an instant
there were cows, a huge herd of cows

and you rode behind them with a white hat, no saddle
a Guatemalan vaquero, and I watched you drive all of them
over a rise in the distance and you were gone.

And I stood in the road which turned to a field and woke up.

The house was quiet, your room empty. The dogs breathed on the floor
and you're still gone, still locked up, probably sleeping
under the inked blackbird sky.

As Christmas Comes

for Gabriel

This morning in fog I wait for the archangel to show himself.
The trumpeting comes in waves but blows into geese and cranes.
In the cold, I'll wait for you to come. Searching for small gods,
they are always in dogs and birds—and often they appear
in people's eyes. At times like this when we want to be together
and share our gifts and we can't, the geese remind us
there are gifts coming all around. Those three wise men
have travelled to deliver them. Let us remember
Christ's small voice in the manger, the love we share
even in the coldest shortest days of our dark winters.

At Dead Horse Point There's Nowhere Else to Go

To go home is to take back a name
—Larry Levis

Come home, son, give yourself back what you need.
Take back what's yours—the sky, the rivers, the ducks
you watch over decoys. Widen the arms and pull in

the neighborhood trees you climbed as a child,
reclaim the nights you smashed with the hammer
of your voice, the hammer of your gun, stars

littered with holes you shot up and take back days she
shot up so much you were left lying against the bank
of her life worried and alone taking care of your love.

Run bare chested down the streets, my son, until you
feel those lungs filling, breath after breath with cool
valley air, until you stand with yourself under the sun

or streetlights. Walk back into the sierras by yourself,
without anything but your own strong hands, the heart
like granite you will reclaim, the wind across bare slopes

of Desolation Wilderness. Swim, feel that cold mountain
water spike your skin. Lift yourself out of that dark lake

after searching, when you've found that name you'll call
yourself, a sound made from the throat of a bird.

Release

The wild horses come down to the river to drink
and eat grassy hummocks along the bank.

Their coats shine in the late summer sun, the canyon
rim towers above us. I know you would love to see them;

you've only heard my stories of these horses.
Three summers ago I watched this canyon burn,

and now the regrowth brings them.
Biology tells us intense heat opens seeds—

even the scorpionweed grows back. When you're out,
the lockdown over, parole is off, we'll float this water,

let your heart run like the river, catch a few fish,
then sit under the stars with a little whiskey

free, where unbranded horses
roam the draws for years.

Notes

1. In the poem "Disappearing Them" the Mission Statement cited is taken directly from the CDCR website. The names, locations, and populations of the California prisons were taken from the CDCR website in November of 2018. The number of employees was taken from the 2019 CDCR Projected Budget.

2. Related to "California Department of Corrections and Rehabilitation: Dial 1 to be Connected to Visiting" the wearing of a bra with an underwire during visiting is strictly prohibited.

3. Visitation at Valley View Conservation Camp" references one of the 39 Conservation Camps run by CDCR in conjunction with Cal Fire which house the inmate firefighter crews. Visiting at these locations is relatively unsupervised and full-contact visiting where visitors are allowed to bring food from outside for visiting and where, in large part, barbecue pits are available for cooking.

4. Inmates at the California Conservation Camps work on crews of 10-12 each with a designated title and job from working a Pulaski or Macleod to the being a Sawyer (running a chainsaw) or Puller.

5. In question 134 of "From the Official National Midterm on

White Oppression and Corrections" WalMart was, at the time of this writing, the largest retailer of firearms in America. SturmRuger is the largest manufacturer of firearms in America. CoreCivic America is formerly the Corrections Corporation of America, owned by the GEO group and part of the largest privatized prison company in the world and traded on the NYSE.

6. Stephon Clark was a young African-American man who was unarmed and shot by police in his grandmother's backyard in Sacramento, CA on March 18, 2018.

7. The California Correctional Center at Susanville is where the inmate training center is located for Northern California Conservation Camps.

8. Access Secure Pak is the privatized company that handles quarterly care package purchasing and delivery for the CDCR.

9. In "Rehabilitation: The Step by Step Process" both the title and the text of the 9 steps are taken from the CDCR website.

10. California's Proposition 57 Sentencing and Parole Guidelines "Allows parole consideration for persons convicted of nonviolent felonies, upon completion of prison term for their primary offense as defined. Authorizes Department of Corrections and Rehabilitation to award sentence credits for rehabilitation, good behavior, or educational achievements" (CaliforniaCourts.ca.gov).

11. In Administrative Segregation, also called AdSeg, inmates are

not allowed to have contact visits and are led to and from visits with guards and in full leg and wrist shackle restraint.

12. Yummy Sandifer was an eleven-year-old boy from the Roseland area of Chicago. He was considered to be a member of the Black Disciples gang and had committed a murder and the killing of his fourteen-year-old neighbor Shavon Dean who was hit by bullets from Sandifer's errant shooting in August of 1994. Yummy Sandifer was then shot, execution-like, by brothers Cragg and Derrick Hardaway ages 16 and 14 who were also considered to be members of the Black Disciples gang.

<u>Acknowledgements</u>

Much gratitude is given to the editors of the journals in which the following poems first appeared.

"Release" *Valparaiso Poetry Review*

"Eclipse" and "Your Cartoon" *Flint Hills Review*

"California Department of Corrections and Rehabilitation: Dial 1 to be Connected to Visiting" and "I Had a Dream About You" *Black Fork Review*

"Sonnet For The Defendant" *Summerset Review*

"Seeing You Even When You're Gone" *Bangalore Review*

"Sometimes You're Still In The House" *Poetry Northwest*

"One Night" and "California Department of Corrections and Rehabilitation: Dial 2 for Inmate Information" *New Ohio Review*

"Fire Season" and "Your Nine" *Atlanta Review*

"California Department of Rehabilitation: Dial 3 To Be Connected To A Representative", "Re-Arrest", "Ekphrasis Of The Yard", and "Ekphrasis Of A Post Visit Strip Search" *Hamilton Stone Review*

I also wish to thank Doug Talley, David Baxley, Kate Gale, Douglas Manuel, Dexter Booth, Marcelo Hernandez Castillo, Kevin Stein, Sandra

Simonds, Christian Kiefer, Michael Spurgeon, Esteban Nunez, and the Anti-Recidivism Coalition.

Without the amazing support of friends and family this collection would not have happened. A very special thank you to Richard and Doris Knorr, Nancy Hirabayashi, Ellyn Hirabayashi, Ben Hirabayashi, and Karissa Hirabayashi, Steve Knorr, Petra Class, and Lucas Class-Knorr, Tim and Sachicko Schell, Al and Terry Garcia, Troy Myers, Steve Plesser, Diane and Steve Wismer, and my lovely family Jessica Cadena, Cruz Alvarez-Machado, Gabriel Knorr, Diego Alvarez-Machado and my wife, Maria Alvarez.

ABOUT THE AUTHOR

Jeff Knorr(b. 1966)
2012-2016 Sacramento Poet Laureate Emeritus

(pictured: J & G)

Jeff Knorr is the author of five books of poetry, *Fire Season* (Flowersong Press) *The Color of a New Country* (Mammoth Books), The *Third Body* (Cherry Grove Collections), *Keeper* (Mammoth Books), and *Standing Up to the Day* (Pecan Grove Press). His other works include *Mooring Against the Tide: Writing Poetry and Fiction* (Prentice Hall); the anthology, *A Writer's Country* (Prentice Hall); and *The River Sings: An Introduction to Poetry* (Prentice Hall). His poetry and essays have appeared widely in literary journals and anthologies including *Chelsea, Poetry Northwest, New Ohio Review, The Journal, North American Review, Hamilton Stone Review, Barrow Street,* and *Like Thunder: Poets Respond to Violence in America.*

Jeff was the Poet Laureate for the city and county of Sacramento from 2012-2016. He has edited, judged, and been a visiting writer for various conferences and festivals. He was the founding co-editor and poetry editor of the *Clackamas Literary Review*. He has also been an invited judge for contests such as the DeNovo First Book Contest, the Willamette Award in Poetry and the Red Rock Poetry Award. He has appeared as a visiting writer at such venues and festivals as Wordstock, University of Pennsylvania's Kelly Writer's House, The Des Moines Festival of Literary Arts, and CSU Sacramento's Summer Writers Conference. He currently directs the River City Writer's Series at Sacramento City College.

Jeff Knorr lives in Sacramento, California and is Professor of literature and creative writing at Sacramento City College.

FLOWERSONG

P R E S S

FlowerSong Press nurtures essential verse from, about, and throughout the borderlands. Literary. Lyrical. Boundless.

Sign up for announcements about
new and upcoming titles at:

www.flowersongpress.com

www.ingramcontent.com/pod-product-compliance
Lightning Source LLC
Chambersburg PA
CBHW011224120626
46545CB00010B/3143